Lawrence Okolo Abutu

The Contemporary West African Economic Development and its Relations with China

Der GRIN Verlag publiziert seit 1998 wissenschaftliche Arbeiten von Studenten, Hochschullehrern und anderen Akademikern als eBook und gedrucktes Buch. Die Verlagswebsite www.grin.com ist die ideale Plattform zur Veröffentlichung von Hausarbeiten, Abschlussarbeiten, wissenschaftlichen Aufsätzen, Dissertationen und Fachbüchern.

Document Nr. V206203

Lawrence Okolo Abutu

The Contemporary West African Economic Development and its Relations with China

GRIN Verlag

Die Deutsche Bibliothek verzeichnet diese Publikation in der Deutschen Nationalbibliografie; detaillierte bibliografische Daten sind im Internet über http://dnb.d-nb.de/ abrufbar.

Dieses Werk sowie alle darin enthaltenen einzelnen Beiträge und Abbildungen sind urheberrechtlich geschützt. Jede Verwertung, die nicht ausdrücklich vom Urheberrechtsschutz zugelassen ist, bedarf der vorherigen Zustimmung des Verlages. Das gilt insbesondere für Vervielfältigungen, Bearbeitungen, Übersetzungen, Mikroverfilmungen, Auswertungen durch Datenbanken und für die Einspeicherung und Verarbeitung in elektronische Systeme. Alle Rechte, auch die des auszugsweisen Nachdrucks, der fotomechanischen Wiedergabe (einschließlich Mikrokopie) sowie der Auswertung durch Datenbanken oder ähnliche Einrichtungen, vorbehalten.

1. Auflage 2012
Copyright © 2012 GRIN Verlag GmbH
http://www.grin.com
Druck und Bindung: Books on Demand GmbH, Norderstedt Germany
ISBN 978-3-656-34636-4

Okolo Abutu Lawrence

PhD Candidate

World Economy

Research School of South-east Asian studies

Department of International Relations

Xiamen University

361005, P.R.China

The Contemporary West African Economic Development and its Relations with China: Evidence from Nigeria

Abstract

The rise of China may well be the most significant trend today redefining the geopolitics of Asia and the world beyond. This reflects in the influx of economic activities from various foreign investors who are attracted to the existence of a market for their products and services in the over 1.3 billion populated country. This also has some connections with the country's investments in other countries such as Sub Saharan Africa. For example Africa supplied 77% of oil, 13 % of metalliferous ore, 3% of cotton, 2% wood, 3% pear and precious stones to Chinese economy, and on the demand side African economy sourced 5% industrial equipment, 7% electrical appliances, 8% telecommunication equipment, 8% transport vehicles, 14% clothing wares, and 16% textiles from the Chinese economy. Essentially, this significant development about China has been linked to its 'open-door policy' which took effect from the 1980s

Although, Sino-Nigerian economic interdependence has grown exponentially over the past few decades, the contemporary waves of diplomatic relations appear to a reasonable extent mutually beneficial. Nigeria's quest for development with an aggressive campaign for FDI as one of the motivating forces has opened the economy which China is seen as an ideal business partner. Accordingly, this paper, through a critical review of the literature examines, and evaluates the opportunities and challenges abound in the nascent economic and trade relationships, and discusses the prospects of the deals for the Chinese, Nigerian, and African socio-economic growth.

Key Words: Africa, China, FDI, Economic, Nigeria, Relations, Investments

Introduction

As China's economy has become more integrated into global markets, its interest and involvement in international affairs particularly West Africa has risen accordingly, resulting in the need for China to develop an articulated and non-contradictory foreign policy to support and protect its growing domestic economy and its economic interests abroad. This process is in stark contrast to the path China has taken during most of its history since its founding in 1949 and the open door policy also reflects the way in which economic growth and foreign policy development go hand in hand as China prominence on the world stage grows tremendously. However, China is the world's most populous country, with more than 1.3 billion people (2012)[1] Consequently, many multinationals including Samsung, Johnson & Johnson, Unilever, Nokia, and Motorola, Wal-Mart, Intel, Carrefour, General Motors, and Volkswagen to mention but few already have their investments in China and are exploring the existing market opportunities such that it is estimated that China received more than $60 billion foreign direct investment in 2003 [2] and reaching RMB 912 billion in 2004.[3] More so, from January to November 2012 alone foreign direct investment in China was worth $ 1013. 96.[4]

More importantly, China-Africa relations started since Mao's presidency. As early as the 1960's China implemented an anti-Western imperialist agenda based on ideological solidarity with other third world countries, China concentrated on building ideological solidarity with other developing countries on repelling western "Imperialism". Currently, China interests evolved into more pragmatic pursuits such as trade, investment, cultural exchange, education, aid and energy. In the Post Cold War era, however, China-Africa relations have significantly shifted from their former ideological focus in to socio-economic and political relations. Equally, West Africa is endowed with many natural resources like oil, gas, wood, diamond, gold, uranium. Nigeria, Mauritania, Niger, Chad, Sudan, Senegal, Conakry Guinea, Mali, Ghana and Bissau Guinea are ones of the most solicited by industrial countries.[5] Currently, China has identified the African continent as a distinct economic and strategic partner. America and Europe consider Africa like a

---

[1] Geohive, Global Statistics/Population Statistics, 27 November, 2012, retrieved from http://www.geohive.com/

[2] Choi, C.J. & Nailer, C. 'The China market and European Companies Prices and Surviving the local competition' *European Business Review*, 2005,' Vol. 17 No 2, pp. 177-190

[3] Strategic Direction, 'Selling of China's rich and not so rich Need to go beyond the luxury market' Vol. 21 No.6,, pp. 5-7, 2005

[4] Invest in China, "Statistics about Utilization of Foreign Investment in China from Jan to Nov 2012" Department of the Ministry of Commerce, China, Retrieved from http://fdi.gov.cn/pub/FDI_EN/Statistics/FDIStatistics/StatisticsofForeignInvestment/t20121219_148155.htm

[5] Omar, Ndao Elhadji, " Investment and Trade between West Africa and China: The Senegalese Case" *Academic Journal of International Business Research*, Vol. 11 No 1, 2012

treasure ruled by opportunists who did not respected democratic rules...the rule of law and that free markets is being challenged by the escalating Chinese influence in Africa and Nigeria in particular.

Hitherto, traditional development partners mainly from Europe and the Americas (U.S. A and Canada) have dominated trade, investment (in terms of foreign direct investment FDI) and grants and financial as well as technical aid to the country. These are governed by various bilateral and regional agreements that exist between these countries and Nigeria. Although Nigeria and these countries have come a long way in their relationship, it is debatable if such has in any significant way assist the country in its quest for development. The relationship appears to be exploitative at least from the trend in the structure and pattern of trade and FDI inflow to the country. This is based on the fact that oil and gas sector dominates the country's exports to the tune of about 98% and FDI inflows to the oil and gas sector accounted for about 40%.[6]

However, China is the second largest economy in the world after United States and her fast-growing economic ties with Africa are attracting considerable attention. The relationship came into the spotlight during the Forum China-Africa Cooperation (FOCAC) in Beijing in November, 2006 and the Annual Meetings of the African Development Bank (AfDB) in Shanghai in May 2007. While the expansion of trade and investment between Africa and China has been generally welcomed, concerns have been expressed about how China's growing might affect African development. But what roles has China exactly played? What drives China's trade and financial involvement in Africa? What are the implications of the relationship for Africa and other developing partners? This paper aims at shedding light on these questions, especially the first two, by examining the Nigerian case.[7]

Apart from the influx of investments into China, it also has several other trade relations with other countries including West African countries such as Nigeria. However, due to the overshadowing effects of the existence of this large consumer market which propels various countries to troop to the Chinese economy, this area is well researched as evident in the literature (see for example Li, Anshan, 2007; *Rooks, 1997;* Lee and Lo, 1998; King and McDaniel, 1998; Parnell, 2002; Jagersma. and van Group, 2003; Kwan *et al.,* 2003; Choi and Nailer, 2005; Chan and Suen, 2005; Robert, 2008) but academic contributions to this nation's investments in other countries are limited and disproportional to those documented about others investing in the country. In the light of the above, this paper explores China-Nigeria economic relations and the significant implications in the form of opportunities and challenges associated with the relationship. Through this, it is hoped that the paper will not only extend our understanding of

---

[6] Abiodun S.B., et al, *China-Nigeria Economic Relations*: Scoping Studies on China-Africa Relations, Trade Policy Research and Training Program (TPRTP) Ibadan, Nigeria, 2008

[7] FOCAC: A Win-Win Formula for Sino-African Relations? 10th October, 2000. Retrieved November 15 2012 from http://www.thebeijingaxis.com/tca/editions/the-china-analyst-jan-2010/64

the economic relations between the two but also deepen the extant literature on the trend of the pacts between China and West African countries among which Nigeria is one.

To be able to achieve this distinct objective above, this paper has been organized in the following form. The next section provides the background information on China-Nigeria relationship and the open door policy; this is followed by China's trade and investment strategies in West Africa which comes immediately before the highlights of China's trade and investment in Nigeria. The next section delves into significant implications of China's FDI on Nigeria's economic development, opportunities and challenges steaming from their relationship come before the conclusion section which features last.

Background Information: China-Nigeria Relationship and the Open Door Policy.

"Good Brothers, Good friends and Good partners" Mr.Borging, the Chinese Ambassador to Nigeria This Day 2007)

China's contemporary engagement with Africa goes back to the founding of modern China in 1949. In the aftermath of the 1955 Bandung Conference, China began to strengthen both political and economic ties with Africa. In the economic sphere, the 1960s in particular witnessed an influx of Chinese businesses to Africa. [8] China's economic progression has resulted in a renewed confidence by its leadership to engage outside world, China is assertively engaging with the global political economy, including that of African continent. The first Sino-African forum (consultative process launched in Beijing, 2000) launched a new era. In the span of 8 years, several hundred cooperation agreements for economic assistance (technical cooperation, project aid and budgetary aid) to African countries were approved.

In 2000, several protocol agreements have been signed to cancel all or partial African debt totaling $10 billion. As a comparison, the initiative favoring the Heavily Indebted Poor Countries (HIPC) Initiative has approved. In the same period the cancellation of the debt of 29 countries of which 25 are African with a total amount of 35 billion US dollars. Moreover, in June 2005 the G8 proposed that three multilateral institutions (the IMF, the International Development Association (IDA) of the World Bank, and the African Development Fund (AfDF))--cancel 100% of their debt claims on countries that have reached, or will eventually reach, the completion point under the joint IMF-World Bank enhanced HIPC Initiative so as to free up additional resources in order to help these countries reach the Millennium Development Goals (MDGs).

Equally, the cooperation framework has been strengthened, as demonstrated by the success of the third Sino-African summit in November 2006, with 48 African countries present. China is

---

[8] Harry Bradman, Africa's Silk Road: China and India's New Economic Frontier, Washington D.C: World Bank, 2007

ahead of other emerging Asian countries like India, Singapore, Thailand, etc. It rivals OECD by announcing in 2005, $10 billion in concessional loans to Africa for the period 2006-2008 periods. Are the recent G8's commitments to Africa related to China's growing interest in Africa? This situation sets the stage for a new balance of power within which Africa will be in a better position to negotiate with external development partners. Trade between China and Africa is set, the emerging complementarily, and finally the Chinese investment in different countries and sectors.[9] Most importantly, February 10th, 2011 was the 40th anniversary of the establishment of diplomatic relations between China and Nigeria. Historically, the diplomatic relations of People's Republic of China and Federal Republic of Nigeria dates back to 10th February, 1971 the two countries bilateral relations have since been witnessing growth in all spheres of their relations.

The frequent high level visits from both sides built up the mutual political trust; this relationship has resulted in several bilateral agreements ranging from economic, trade, culture, educational ties and many more. Equally, it is reported that about 20,000 Chinese live in Nigeria especially at the major economic zones of the country namely, Abuja, Kano, and Lagos. In August 2001 both countries signed an agreement on investment promotion and protection; in April 2002 they signed the agreement for avoidance of double taxation and the prevention of fiscal evasion with respect to taxes on income. And three months later (July, 2002) the agreements on consular affairs, cooperation on strengthening management of Narcotic drugs, psychotropic substances, and diversion of precursor chemical, and tourism cooperation were signed by both countries. Apparently these ties have strengthened their economic relationships as both economies experience economic reforms and developments.[10]

Fundamentally, China remains the most populated country in the world with over 1.3 billion people.[11] While Nigeria is ranked 7th in the list of most populated countries in the world with over 168 million people estimated by United Nations in December, 2012.[12] However, the cooperation of the two countries in international affairs has enjoyed broader space. In the early 1970s when China-Nigeria established diplomatic relations along with other independent African countries the focus had largely been on international support for China's One China principle to

---

[9] Omar, Ndao Elhadji, " Investment and Trade between West Africa and China: The Senegalese Case" *Academic Journal of International Business Research, Vol. 11 No 1, 2012*

[10] Ayantuni G& Ayodele C.O, Strategic implications of China's Pacts with Sub-Saharan African Countries: The Case of Nigeria, *International Journal.org, p.2*

[11] National Bureau of Statistics of China, April 28 2011. Retrieved 10 December 2011 from http://www.stats.gov.cn/english/newsandcomingevents/t20110428_402722237.htm

[12] Geohive, Global Statistics/Population Statistics, 27 November, 2012, Retrieved from http://www.geohive.com/

sidetrack Taiwan's ascendancy, and its gaining of permanent seat at UNO Security Council.[13] The friendship and international support has laid the foundation for continued cooperation between China and Africa in which Nigeria's role was significant. However, going by Goldman Sachs predictions in 2005 that the future outlooks for the two economies, China and Nigeria can be considered blissful according to this renowned institution's account, the two nations by 2050 shall be regarded as the largest economies on different plains; Monye posited that China will be the largest economy in the world while Nigeria will be Africa's prime. This is not only scenario where the two nations are in tandem with each other with respect to other nations of the world. [14] Equally, Nigeria's relations with China have grown in the last decade from the limited and intermittent contact that marked the immediate post-independence era to an increasingly complex and expansive engagement. While, like most other African countries in the 1960s and 70s, Nigeria viewed China as a nonaligned developing country, it did little to foster business or even special diplomatic relations with the Asian giant. Nigeria's trade focused primarily on European and North American countries, which proclaimed themselves development partners. China's own economic and political challenges made it an unlikely development partner at that time. Following Deng Xiaoping's reform policies of the 1970s and 80s, China's dramatic growth and modernization, and attendant industrial, energy, and market expansion needs, brought it into greater contact with Africa. Its new expanded presence offered a partnership seen by many stakeholders as an alternative model to Western relationships.[15]

After they established diplomatic ties in 1971, internal crises faced by both countries reduced the pace of economic integration like Nigeria, the trade policy since 1960 witnessed extreme swings from high protectionism from the West in the first few decades after independence and also placed high restrictions on the importation of capital goods that could have enhanced local industries like machineries to boost agricultural production. The relation of the two countries grows closer as a result of international isolation and condemnation of Nigeria's military regimes 1970-1998.[16]

More so, by 1960-1998 the governments of newly independent Nigeria adopted a broadly pro-Western stance, and while it did not actively support Taiwan, it also did not seek relations with China. Chinese Premier Zhou En-Lai's 10-country trip to Africa in 1963 did not include Nigeria, and a Chinese delegation that visited Nigeria in 1964 seeking the establishment of diplomatic ties was sent away empty-handed. Unlike other African countries that did draw close to China,

---

[13] Tull DM, " China's Engagement in Africa: Scope, Significance and Consequence ", *Journal of Modern Africa Studies*, Vol.44 No.3, 2006, pp.459-479

[14] Goldman Sachs, How Solid are the BRICs? Global Economics Papers No 134, 2005, p.8 retrieved from http://www.goldmansachs.com/our-thinking/topics/brics/brics-reports-pdfs/how-solid.pdf on 4 Dec. 2012

[15] Adeolu O. Adewuyi, et al, Impact of China-Africa Trade Relations: The Case of Nigeria. The African Economic Research Consortium, 2010 p. 3

[16] Ibid p.4

Nigeria never received gifts of imposingly built sports stadiums or government ministry buildings from the Chinese government during this era.[17]

China's post-Mao rulers, led by Deng Xiaoping, adopted a different economic development strategy called "reform and opening." Reform meant changes in the domestic economic and administrative systems, especially freeing the peasants from the communes so they could farm as families or engages in local industry and freeing industrial enterprises to compete in a market environment. Opening meant joining the global economy, allowing foreign trade and investment to flourish. China has now become one of the world's major trading nations and is poised to join the World Trade Organization which sets the rules for the global trading economy during this period [18]

China's Trade and Investment Strategies in West Africa

One China Policy: The economic and diplomatic relationships between China and each African country have been largely determined by the position of the African nations regarding the sovereignty of China relatively to the position of Taiwan. Before now, China has enjoyed the support of many African countries on this issue and other diplomatic issues, and this has tremendously been responsible for the relationships between China and some African countries like Nigeria. For example, the independent African nations largely voted for China to obtain one of the five permanent seats on United Nations (UN) Security Council in 1971 on the recognition of "One China" to the detriment of Taiwan; China secured 26 votes of African nations out of the 76 votes that sealed its election into the council.[19] Inherently, this singular support and recognition of "One China" had to a large extent determined China relationship with many African countries.

Win–win Partnership: The win-win partnership in the FOCAC agreement demonstrates the mutual benefits for China and the trade partners in the Sub-Sahara Africa in the new economic relationship. In the same vein, it primarily shows that, as the Chinese companies carry out the raw materials exploration, commensurate compensation and development would be carried out in the local areas or the nation at large, however, a win for China and a win for Africa governments. Thus, China is seen to be extending goodwill to develop constructive trade relationships. [20] On a larger scale, the implication of the win-win partnership is to create an economic cooperation and a new international diplomatic and economic order that strengthens a long-undermined South-

---

[17] Utomi P, China-Nigeria, Washington, Centre for Strategic and International Studies, 2008, p. 40.

[18] Ibid p. 40

[19] Atlas on Regional Integration in West Africa, *Africa and China,* ECOWAS-SWAC/OECD, December 2006

[20] Pang, C. K., et al, "Doing business in China – the art of war?", *International Journal of Contemporary Hospitality Management*, 10/7, 272–282, 1998.

South relationship.[21] More so, the intent is to create accessibility to African exported products in the Chinese market and vice-versa, and to create economic cooperation in other spheres of economy like, technology, agriculture and infrastructural development.

Non-Interference in the local politics: China builds its economic relationship with African countries and other developing rich-resource economies that have become sources for its raw materials on the political ideology of non-interference in the local politics of the trading partners. This to a greater extent is contrary to 'Washington Consensus".[22] More importantly, China's economic interest and investment is considered far more important than the internal conflict or political instability, or autocratic ruler ship in the host country, hence China supports any government in power to protect its foreign investment. It is observed that the only countries where China has become the pre-eminently ally and commercial partner are those that have been ostracized by the West, such as Myanmar and Sudan.[23] A similar development is that of China's relationship with Zimbabwe in spite of the international call to bring the present government to check through economic sanctions to restore peace and stability to the country. Thus, China's investment and economic support along with diplomatic relationship has made pariah states to defy international pressure. More so, the need to tie economic aids and other economic largesse, and even bilateral agreements to respect for human rights and democracy in order to create accountability and responsibility in governance among some African economies may be truncated with the China's policy of non interference in internal affairs.[24]

China's Trade and Investment in Nigeria

The relationship between Nigeria and China has helped Nigeria shed its colonial leanings towards the West, and look at Asian alternatives. Nigeria's population which is over 160 million has benefited tremendously from Chinese interest not just economic affairs, but also in the fields of technology, education, culture, health. Nigeria has benefitted tremendously from China's assistance in putting its railway network back on track. The modernization of Nigeria's one track rail to standard gauge rail though under construction is said to be worth $ 8.3 billion in the first phase which China would financed and refurbished about $ 2.3 billion as loan in the project. It has helped extend the network into the interiors of the country, thereby enhancing connectivity. To top all, China also provided the funds for the entire project. The completed project will ease transportation of goods throughout Africa and perishable goods like fruits and

---

[21] Shinn D.H, "An Opportunistic Ally: China's Increasing Involvement in Africa", *Harvard Business Review*, Vol. 29 No. 2, 2007, pp. 52.

[22] Policy Insights, "From Old-Donor Debt Relief to Emerging Lenders in Africa" No. 57, 2008, http://www.oecd.org/dev/insights

[23] The Economist, *A Ravenous Dragon: A Special Report on China's Quest for Resources*, March 15, 2008, pp. 1-18

[24] Tull DM, " China's Engagement in Africa: Scope, Significance and Consequence ", *Journal of Modern Africa Studies*, Vol.44 No.3, 2006, pp.459-479

vegetables would be able to reach their destination in a far fresher state from the northern cities to the southern ones.[25]

Additionally, the figure 1.1 below shows a comprehensive outline of bilateral trade relations between China and Nigeria from 2000 to 2010. Before then, the bilateral trade between China and Nigeria has come a long way; historically in 1969 its total value was recorded at Great British Pound (GBP) 2.3 million, increasing to GBP 5 million in 1970 and by 1971 it rose to GBP 10.3 million. However, right from the early stages, the terms of trade were in Chinese favor with GBP 4 million of trade recorded in 1970 derived from Chinese textile exports to Nigeria.[26] By 1994 recorded bilateral trade had risen to $90 million. Although a significant increase on the trade levels of two decades earlier, this was still a very low figure or number. Yet bilateral trade more than doubled to $ 210 million in 1995, and had climbed to $830 million by 2000. While some of this increase was precipitated by Nigerian exports to China, Nigeria exports to China were worth $60 million in 1995, but $ 293 million in 2000, a nearly five-fold increase yet the terms of the trade favored China, whose exports represented about 73 percent of the bilateral trade total in 1995 and 68 percent of the total in 2000. Also, China's trade and investment relations intensified after 2000 and there have been a corresponding dramatic development in the bilateral trade level since then. Bilateral trade in 2008 was worth $7.3 billion, almost nine times its level in 2000. China's exports represented 93% of the bilateral trade total in 2010.[27]

---

[25] Utomi, P, China and Nigeria. Washington, Center for Strategic and International Studies, 2008.p. 42

[26] Bukarambe, B. Nigeria-China Relations: The Unacknowledged Sino-dynamics: in Ogwu, (ed), New Horizons for Nigeria in World affairs, Lagos: Nigeria Institute of International Affairs 2005, p 235

[27] Ibid, p. 236

Figure 1.1 Trades between China and Nigeria, 2000-2010

West Africa here includes ECOWAS countries plus Chad and Mauritania

Source: Margaret Egbula & Qi Zheng, *China and Nigeria: A Powerful South-South Alliance*, 2011, p. 6

Around 90 percent of Nigeria exports to China are oil products, which is in line with oil products share of Nigeria's total export value. China by contrast, has exported an ever-growing range of products to Nigeria. Furthermore, by 2008 the single biggest export to Nigeria recorded imported products by value were electrical apparatus for line telephony, and closely followed by motorcycles and less closely by electric generators, which there were high demand in Nigeria because of its poor electricity supply. By 2005, 7.1 percent of the nation's total recorded imports came from China.[28] In addition, in 2009, the bilateral trade volume increased to $6.37 billion. In 2010, trade between the two countries was worth $ 7.8 billion. In 2011, Nigeria was the 4th largest trading partner of China in Africa and in the first 8 month of 2012 it was the 3rd[29]. In the same vein, in 2011 China-Nigeria bilateral trade volume hit $10billion but the figure for 2012 is not yet confirmed. The accumulated Chinese actual investment in Nigeria reached US $4.14

---

[28] Gregory, M.S, *Elephant, Ants and Superpowers: Nigeria's Relations with China; South African Institute of International (SAIIA) Affairs, Perspectives Global Insight*, 2009, p.10

[29] Bbc news online, "China Pledges $ 20 Credit for Africa at Summit" Retrieved 28 December, 2012 from www.bbc.co.uk/news/world-asiachina-18897451

billion in December 2006 and jumped to US $7.55 billion in 2010, up 82%. Furthermore, China's exports to Nigeria by product, 2010 alone: vehicles 11%, electrical equipment 10%, agro-food products 3%, industrial machinery 9%, textile materials 9%, telecommunication equipments 9% while China's imports from Nigeria by products, 2010 were: petroleum and gas 87%, leather manufactures 3%, metals 7% .[30]

The Implication of China's FDI on Nigeria's Economic Development

A lot of policy makers and academics contend that foreign direct investment (FDI) can have significant effects on a host country's development effort.[31] In addition to direct capital financial it supplies, FDI can be a source of valuable technology know-how while fostering linkages with local firms, which can help jumpstart an economy. Based on these debates, industrialized and developing nations have offered incentives to encourage FDI in their economies. Presently, however, the special advantages of FDI and particularly the kinds of incentives offered to foreign firms in practice have begun to be questioned. Fueling this augment is that empirical evidence for FDI generating positive spillovers for host nations is ambiguous at the micro and macro levels.[32] In another development, China's investments abroad are booming despite an overall decline globally in foreign direct investment (FDI) following the 2008 financial crisis. That trend in Chinese investments abroad is likely to continue, since China's huge foreign exchange reserves are an increasing source of mobile capital and is a key part of China's official government policy. The receipts from China's existing global investments, combined with mounting trade surpluses, have made China the world's largest capital-surplus economy. [33] Although China's outward direct investment (ODI) is still small relative to its massive inward FDI, China's overseas companies have been gaining momentum in moving international capital, investing across a broad spectrum of sectors ranging from natural resources to manufacturing to telecommunications and many others. As China's economy continues to grow, China faces shortages in almost all raw materials, particularly in oil, iron ore, aluminum, and uranium, and it must therefore build trade linkages with Australia, Russia, Brazil, Nigeria and other resource-rich countries to secure supplies.[34]

---

[30] Margaret Egbula & Qi Zheng, China and Nigeria: A Powerful South-South Alliance, 2011, pp. 6-8

[31] Markusen J, "The Boundaries of Multinational Enterprises and the Theory of International Trade" *Journal of Economic Perspectives* 9: 1995, pp. 169-89

[32] Aitken, B.J & Harrison A, "Do Domestic Firms Benefit from Direct Foreign Investment? Evidence from Venezuela" American Economic Review 89: 1999, Pp. 605-618

[33] Nargiza Salidjanova, Policy Analyst for Economic and Trade Issues, Going Out: An Overview of China's Outward Foreign Direct Investment, 2011, p 1 Retrieved 21 Nov. 2012 from http://www.uscc.gov/researchpapers/2011/GoingOut.pdf

[34] Leonard K. Cheng & Zihui Ma, "China's Outward FDI: Past and Future," in Proceedings of the NBER (National Bureau of Economic Research) Conference on China's Growing Role in World Trade (Chicago: University of Chicago Press, 2007, p. 5. http://nber15.nber.org/books_in_progress/china07/cwt07/cheng.pdf.

For many years, China's economic engagement with Nigeria was limited. Relations stayed at the government-to-government level, consisting of aid agreements and development projects. However, relations have since greatly expanded into the private sector, with investment often directly encouraged by both the Nigerian and Chinese governments. The Chinese business presence, previously limited to the venturing of Hong Kong textile producers and steel processors, is increasingly being replaced by big commitments from Chinese financial institutions. The climate in Nigeria now features Nigerian consultants marketing themselves as having the capacity to manage project financing from China. The acquisition of a stake in Standard Chartered Bank, one of Africa's leading banks, as well as a stake in IBTC-Chartered Bank in Nigeria, by one of China's largest banks, has significantly raised China's investment profile. As Chinese banks continue to support Chinese enterprise in Nigeria, a surge in the level of business involvement is expected to grow sharply.[35]

Infrastructural Development: China involvement in trade and economic relationships with Sub-Sahara Africa equally involves infrastructural development across the region. This cut across electricity projects, government buildings, sport facilities and transport - railway, road networks, airport and the likes. Infrastructural development is part of the strategic cooperation in the FOCAC meeting in November, 2006. These contracted projects mostly involve "construction projects of China's diplomatic missions and projects financed by sources other than the Chinese government but undertaken by Chinese contractors with approval of China's Ministry of Commerce".[36] According to White (2006), "in Nigeria, oil rights secured earlier this year are linked to plans to channel $4 billion into refineries, power and other infrastructure. A deal was recently reached with a Chinese contractor for $8.3 billion project to rebuild the dilapidated colonial-era railway between Lagos and the Northern Nigerian of Kano, in the first stage of the ambitious 20-year rail modernization plan". Also, there is a joint venture between Chinese Oil and Natural Gas Corporation and Indian multi-national company L. N. Mittal Group plans to invest $6 billion in railways, oil refinery and power in exchange for rights to drill oil in Nigeria.[37] Furthermore, $200 million is projected by Chinese firm in preferential buyers' credit for Nigeria's first communication satellite. These contracted projects received the blessing of the Federal government of Nigeria to strengthen the economic relationship with China and to accelerate the infrastructural development in Nigeria which to a large extent has been the bane of formidable socio-economic development of the economy for some time. By and large, official Chinese statistics show the sum of 'contracted projects labour consultation' and 'design consultation' in Africa is being less than $2 billion in 2001.

---

[35] Utomi, P., China and Nigeria, Washington, Center for Strategic and International Studies, 2008, p.44

[36] Wang J, "What Drives China's Growing Role in Africa? " *IMF Working Paper*, Vol. 7, No. 211, 2007, p.8

[37] Bello W, "China Eyes Africa: The New Imperialism? *Multinational Monitor*, Vol. 28 No.1, 2007, pp.23

The impacts of Chinese FDI on the oil sector: The Nigerian government depends heavily on joint-venture operations to fund oil exploration and development. Joint ventures account for approximately 95%t of the country's crude production. The largest joint venture involves Shell Petroleum Development Company (SPDC) of Nigeria Ltd (30 percent); Nigerian National Petroleum Company (NNPC) (55 percent); Elf Petroleum Nigeria Limited (EPNL) (10 percent); and AGIP (5 percent) Sinopec of China. Together these companies produce nearly half of Nigeria's crude oil, with a daily output of approximately 1.1 million barrels.[38] In addition, ExxonMobil currently produces approximately 570,000 bpd in Nigeria and plans to invest $11 billion in the country's oil industry between 2003 and 2011 to increase production to 1.2 million bpd. The majority of Nigeria's oil is exported to markets in the U.S. and Western Europe, with Asia becoming increasingly significant as well.[39]

In the same development, Nigeria is number one oil producer in Africa and the world's tenth largest oil producers.[40] 80 percent of the government's revenues come from the oil sector. As of December 2012, Nigeria's oil reserves estimated at 37 billion barrels. Historically, China had been shut out of Nigeria by Western firms. However, through patience and hard working, political prowess, and technological contributions to the nation, such as promising to build and launch a communication satellite for Nigeria by 2007 which finally materialized in 2011, Chinese firms are gaining a foothold in the industry. In December 2004 Sinopec and NNPC signed an agreement to develop Oil Mining Lease (OML) 64 and 66, located in the waters of the Niger Delta in South Nigeria. OML 64 has drilled five exploration wells with one well encountering hydrocarbon resources. OML 66 has drilled 18 exploration wells with 12 encountering hydrocarbon resources. In October 2004 Xinhua reported that Nigeria would need $10 billion annually in the next five years to meet its target for oil reserves of 40 billion barrels by 2010 and to eliminate gas flaring by 2008.[41] The Nigerian government signed a memorandum of understanding with China National Offshore Oil Corp. (CNOOC) to identify suitable net upstream oil and gas assets that would be integrated into the downstream projects, including refining, power generation, petrochemicals and fertilizer, in partnership with local industry players.[42] In July 2005, CNOOC and NNPC signed an $800 million contract that will

---

[38] "Nigeria," Energy Information Administration, Country Analysis Briefs, November 24, 2012, from <http://www.eia.doe.gov>

[39] Cindy H, China's Oil Rush in Africa: Energy Security July 2006 p 10, Retrieved 24 Nov. 2012 from http://www.iags.org/chinainafrica.pdf

[40] CNBC, The world's 15 Biggest Oil Producers, retrieved from http://www.cnbc.com/id/41887743/The_World_s_15_Biggest_Oil_Producers?slide=7 10 December, 2012.

[41] "China, Nigeria Sign Oil Development Agreement," China Daily, 19 December 2004, <http://www.chinadaily.com/cn> Accessed August 18, 2012

[42] Nigeria Needs $10 B Investment Annually for O&G Industry," Xinhua News Agency, 11 October 2004, <http://www.rigzone.com> Accessed 25 December 2012

guarantee China receives 30,000 bpd for one year. Most recently, and having the most profound impact, was a mutually beneficial deal between China and Nigeria recently signed by President Hu. In exchange for a $4 billion investment on infrastructure, CNPC was given first refusal rights on four oil blocks. However, through continued hardworking and geopolitical prowess, the pendulum has been swinging in China's direction. Nigeria has reportedly favored Asian investors, who are more willing to offer vitally needed infrastructure developments in exchange for drilling rights. With time, China could easily replace some of these Western firms when drilling licenses come up for renewal.

The impacts of Chinese FDI on the communication sector: Nigeria's telecoms market has undergone massive growth, which has resulted in economic development. However, Nigeria is considered one of the major markets for telecoms business opportunities in the world. [43] In addition, the telecoms sector was deregulated, foreign investment was encouraged, and licenses were introduced as part of the government's liberalization policy. Along with the introduction of the Global System for Mobile communication, GSM service providers were selectively granted licenses and Nigerian Telecommunications Limited (NITEL) was set in the process of privatization. This led to substantial growth in the communication sector, where prior to the reforms, the ICT penetration in Nigeria was considerably very low with less than 1% of the population having access to a telephone due to high connection charges and problems.[44] Equally, the government's deregulation of the telecoms sector effectively increased competition in the market, distinctively reduced tariffs, improved countrywide network coverage and provided employment opportunities in the nation.

Private investors in Nigeria's telecoms sector has increased from about Naira (NGN) 1.09 billion (US$ 50 million) to over NGN 3,865 billion (US$ 25 billion) by 2010. Furthermore, by the end of the year 2010, 65 Nigerians out of every 100 had a phone, which suggests that though the majorities are connected, there is still some opportunity to be had in the sector. The market is expected to continue growing, as the total number of mobile subscribers is expected to reach 90.47 million people by the end of 2011. Subsequent licensing by the Nigerian Communication Commissions (NCC) has given GSM network providers the responsibility of providing fixed and mobile telephony, and Internet and broadband access, thus increasing their range of services.[45]
The Nigerian telecoms sector has become the largest generator of foreign direct investment after the nation's oil and gas industry.

---

[43] Alabi, G A, 'Telecommunications in Nigeria', University of Pennsylvania African Studies Centre, March 1996, Retrieved 25 July 2012 from http://www.africa.upenn.edu/ECA/aisi_inftl.html

[44] Rafeeat Aliyu, Chinese and Indian Investment in the African Telecoms Sector, Consultancy Africa Intelligence, 2011, pp. 1-2

[45] Tella S A et al, 'Telecommunications Infrastructure and Economic Growth: Evidence from Nigeria', Paper submitted at a conference entitled "Sector-led growth in Africa and implications for development", Commissioned by UNIDEP and AFEA, November 2007 Retrieved 26 December 2012 from, http://www.unidep.org/Release3/Conferences/Afea_2007/IDEP-AFEA-07-17.pdf

Also, One of the contributions of Chinese FDI to Nigeria's economic development is in communication, the very large Chinese telecoms provider of telecoms equipment and network solutions, Zhongxing Telecommunication Equipment Corporation (ZTE) has a presence in the Nigerian mobile telecoms market, mostly through cooperation with existing GSM and code division multiple access (CDMA) operators in the country. ZTE established a subsidiary company in Nigeria in 1999 - the same year that the Nigerian telecoms sector was deregulated - and reportedly regards Nigeria as "key for their African business activities in the next couple of years.[46] Huawei Technologies, another significant Chinese corporation, also established its operations in Nigeria in 1999 and boasts that more than 50% of its employees are local.[47] Huawei provides telecoms solutions and possesses knowledge in telecoms network infrastructure, software, devices, and professional services. Currently, Huawei has a vantage position in the Nigerian telecoms market as a hardware provider in cooperation with telecoms operators in Nigeria.[48] As part of a partnership agreement with Nigeria's Ministry of Communication, Huawei deployed CDMA450 wireless technology across Nigeria. While China Development Bank will provide Nigeria with a loan of US$200 million for this project, Huawei has committed an additional US$20 million intended for manufacturing investment. More so, Huawei demonstrated their commitment to the local Nigerian community, by invested 10 million USD to build Hawaii's Nigerian Training Center (HNTC), at which more than 800 people have undergone training as of February 2006. Furthermore, Huawei has cooperated with several universities in Nigeria to provide training for their teachers. Finally, the telecoms industry in Nigeria has contributed to the economy in terms of employment generation and foreign direct and private investment, it still remains to be seen how these companies will improve Nigeria's economy in the long-term.

Other composition of Chinese FDI in Nigeria: China Civil Engineering Construction Company also known as (CCECC) has tremendous impact in the development of Nigeria's construction. One of the first projects of CCECC was a $ 4.8 million, 71 kilometer rehabilitation of the Papalanto-Lagos expressway in 2000-01, which was followed by much more substantial contract, a $ 50.5 million, 5000 unit athletes' village for the eight annual All-African Games in Abuja, which was completed in August 2003.[49] CCECC rehabilitated the Ikot Akpaden-okoroette road in 2003-04 for $ 5.7 million, built a new $ 16.7 million cooperate headquarters for the Nigerian Communication Commission (NCC) in Abuja in 2003-2005, and is the main construction company at the Lekki Free Trade Zone near Lagos. More so, the federal

---

[46] 'Chinese telecommunication magnate to expand Nigerian market', Xinhua, 25 August 2011, Retrieved 26 July 2012 from http://news.xinhuanet.com

[47] Gregory Mthembu-Salter, Elephants, Ants and Superpowers: Nigeria's Relations with China. *South African Institute of International Affairs: African Perspectives' Global insights,* September 2009. P 17

[48] See Huawei website http://www.huawei.com/africa/en/catalog.do?id=312 Accessed on 26 November 2012

[49] See >http://www.ccecc.com.cn/english/2006-3/200633090711.htt>. Accessed 3 Dec. 2012

government of Nigeria awarded the rehabilitation contract on the 448km lagos-Jebba rail track to the CCECC worth N 12.1 billion. Another prominent Chinese construction company active in Nigeria is China Geo-Engineering Corporations (GGC) which has been present in the country since the 1980s when it started digging boreholes. It has been involved in numerous projects which include Kebbi Airport, a major water supply project in Gombe State, the road from Kano to Maduguri and many other smaller routes and construction of the Sabke dam. More so, excluding South Africa, Nigeria received the largest inward Chinese foreign direct investment (FDI) flows during the period 2003 to 2009 US$ 916 million. More so, Chinese FDI contributed 0.46 percent, 0.13 percent and 0.11 percent annual GDP growth in 2007, 2008 and 2009 respectively. However, it was able to have such a large impact on Nigerian GDP growth despite it being the second largest economy in Sub-Saharan Africa (at 18% of SSAGDP) due to Nigeria low capital stock to GDP ratio. The largest capital share of Nigeria also plays a part in this.[50]

Opportunities

China has emerged as an economic powerhouse (projected to have the largest economy in the world in a little over a decade) and is taking an ever-increasing role on the world stage. At the first FOCAC Ministerial Conference China announced it would reduce or cancel African countries' debts to China, and encouraged Chinese companies to invest in Africa and train professionals for Africa. At the second FOCAC ministerial conference in 2003, China pledged to increase aid to Africa, enhance cooperation in the sphere of human resources development and give zero-tariff treatment to some of the exported products from the Least Developed Countries (LDCs) in Africa with diplomatic ties with China. However, there have been a number of cases of tripartite cooperation, including the South- South Cooperation Programme run through the Food and Agriculture Organization's Food Security Programme. China contributed 514 experts and technicians to Nigeria under the first five-year phase of this programme. That was from 2003 to 2007.

China has shown a tremendous commitment towards Africa and Nigeria's development in their "Win-Win" relationship. Chinese aid to Africa has been disseminated in three ways: Debt relief and loans as well as infrastructure and Human development. As part of China's contribution towards overcoming the infrastructural gap in Nigeria , its Export Credit Guarantee Agency known as SINOURE provided a whooping $40 to 50 billion to Nigeria to address the problem. Nigeria's government confirmed that it secured loan a $ 900 million from China after she signed the loan agreement with the Export-Import Bank of China; the China loaned was part of the larger borrowing package of $1.54 billion approved by Nigerian senate. China has provided a generous technical assistance; and China's debt relief in Africa has been mostly the cancelation of free loans and to a lesser extent the write-off of concessional loans. For example, in 2005,

---

[50] Gregory Mthembu-Salter, Elephants, Ants and Superpowers: Nigeria's Relations with China. *South African Institute of International Affairs: African Perspectives' Global insights,* September 2009

China loan $ 8 billion to Nigeria, Mozambique and Angola for infrastructural and industrial development.

Also, Beijing commitment in the area of education; PRC has been building schools, hosting training seminars and granting full and partial scholarships to thousands of Africans and Nigerian's students every year. Similarly, China is affiliated with the Nnamadi Azikiwe University, Awka to provide Chinese language teaching to Nigeria students and Institute of Chinese language and the University of Lagos. Under this scheme, the Chinese government provides the opportunity for the training of the university's staff to study Mandarin in China ranging from undergraduate to doctorate levels. This scheme is also characterized by frequent exchanges of cultural tropes and students. Beijing demonstrated it further in her pursuance of "Win-Win" relationship with African countries

Challenges

As Beijing continues in transaction with Nigeria, the opportunities discussed above are existent. However, there are other areas of challenges which are of utmost significance and call for attention to maintain the pacts. These are discussed in turn in this section.

Funds from China are frequently far below what is portrayed in the media. For example, although reports about Chinese loans in Nigeria mentioned figures like $5 billion or more, according to Nigeria's debt management officials, China had actually provided only a total of $589 million in five separate loans to Nigeria between 2000 and 2009. The interest rate of these loans varied between three percent and six percent. The grace periods ranged from three and six years, and maturities were between eight and 12 years. Furthermore, in 2007, China Eximbank made an offer to Nigeria of a $2 billion line of credit at a very competitive commercial rate to finance infrastructure projects in connection with preferential access to oil blocks. Separately, the Chinese government offered Nigeria a $500 million preferential line of export credit for use in areas to be determined between the two sides. There was no ODA involved in the discussions or in the package. Some observers have stated that the $2 billion was offered on concessional terms while other analysts disagree. In the same vein, an exclusive April 2009 interview with the former Nigerian president, Yar'Adua, printed in The Guardian (Lagos), commented that he had also believed it to be concessional, until he visited China and held discussions. He is quoted as having said: "When I visited China and we discussed, I was told this 500 million dollars was given on concessionary rate from the Chinese government but the $2 billion dollars was given at commercial rate from the Chinese Exim Bank."The proposed "infrastructure-for-oil" deal fell through. The framework agreements and memoranda of understanding on both lines of credit would normally have expired after two years, although the Chinese government later extended the $500 million preferential export credit offer until 2010, possibly to assist in the resuscitation of a large contract awarded to a Chinese construction company to rebuild the Lagos-Kano railway, but later suspended after a change of government or after the death of the president.

Recently, Nigerian Customs and Excise department reported the seizure of 30 trailers load of contraband goods and the extent of gross violation of Nigerian import and export laws by Chinese traders in various 'China towns'. This development is antithetical to the economic development of Nigeria. Also, in the Southern Africa region, the expiration of AGOA (Africa Growth and Opportunity Act) established by the US, which was highly exploited by Chinese textiles firms, has turned the Southern African market to dumping ground for Chinese firms that have relocated back. Malone (2008) observed that China in its desperate attempt has found Africa as a new market and perfect destination to sell its cheap and shoddy products due to poor and non-existent health and safety rules and framework in many countries in the continent. This singular development has led to closure of many textiles firms in the region and the industry experiencing high unemployment rate in recent time. The need for insistence on Chinese firms to obey the import and export regulations cannot be compromised in order to achieve sustained economic growth.

CONCLUSION

This paper explores the presently thriving China-Nigeria bilateral economic relations. Consequently, it highlights the associated implications and challenges. As a further contribution to the extant literature in this area, the following noteworthy conclusions are made. The relationship between the two countries have huge current and potential benefits to both countries and Africa as a continent as it further creates more favourable environment for business ties between China and Africa.

Also, there is a need for Nigeria to diversify exports to China and other developed nations by increasing exports value added through moving from exportation of pure raw materials to processing. This is considered imperative to accelerate technological development in Nigeria. Invariably, avoidance of unequal partnership is strategic to Nigeria in the bilateral agreement, and opportunity to explore the special tariff (Special Preferential Tariff Treatment – SPTT) on African exports recently introduced by Chinese government with processed and manufactured products rather than pure raw materials alone. Thus, while Nigeria will enjoy sustainable and profitable economic relationship with China by increasing the value-added of its exported mineral resources to China as suggested, it is equally relevant for it to effectively manage the importation of Chinese products to avoid 'killing' growing local infant industries that dominate the small and medium scale sector in the Nigeria. This is especially so, as there is a view among many Africans that the uncontrolled influx of China's products undermines job markets in Africa.

Conclusively, Chinese investments can be found in a wide variety of sectors, including so-called fragile states and projects that Western investors have seemingly deemed too risky, the willingness of Chinese expatriates to accept the same living conditions offered to local workers

should be seen as an opportunity rather than a threat. Finally, China-Nigeria: the future as foretold by Goldman Sachs, that the two nations are headed in the same direction but different destinations, China will be at the zenith of the world economy while Nigeria will be seated at the helm of a continental economy, Africa in 2050.

Recommendations

Nigeria's first priority lies in developing the capacity to better manage its own policies towards China's engagement. Nigeria needs to realize that China's engagement gives it an ample opportunity to distinctively expand its development and articulate a more comprehensive plan that addresses its long term needs. More so, Nigerian government should avoid short-term fixes and front-loaded deals with the Chinese and move beyond arrangements that should concentrate solely on the petroleum sector.

The quality and standard of goods should be checked; the two governments should utilize their own talent by pooling together leading officials, through various institutions involved with quality control policies and implementation. The facts that Nigerian businessmen have been accused of ordering the same inferior goods that Nigerian citizen have complained about demonstrates that stronger value needed. Nigeria needs business leaders who are ready to press for reform and advocate the added value of transparent business practices. However, at times, China exports substandard products to Nigeria's market there by giving them bad image; China needs to improve her products before exporting it as quality assurance is an important part of building a reputable brand and wining the heart of customers.

The Nigerian government should consider adopting policies that create a capable, vibrant and reliable private sector. These policies should be aimed at strengthening good governance, sustainable development and promoting economic growth, without a focused and dynamic private sector no society can move on, not minding the amount of assistance or aid.

Definition of Foreign Aid should be clear; Chinese foreign aid to Nigeria and Africa as a whole is complicated. People's Republic of China ought to be precise what they deem Foreign Aid, ODA, Trade and Investment specific definitions and its implementation should be formulated. Nigeria for example, between 2000 and 2008, Chinese Engineering Companies reported earning a sum of $ 6.1 billion in revenue from their numerous projects implemented in Nigeria. One well-known Chinese contractor had embarked more than two dozen projects for various branches of Nigeria government over the past decade. In comparison, China's ODA commitments to Nigeria are relatively very small. Surprisingly, estimated to total less than $ 220 million between 2000 and 2008 (or $ 440 million a preferential $ 200 million credit for a communication satellite

is counted as development assistance)[51]. For clarity, economic cooperation data should not be seen as aid.

References

Ayantuni G& Ayodele C.O, Strategic implications of China's Pacts with Sub-Saharan African Countries: The Case of Nigeria, *International Journal.org, p.2*

Alabi, G A, 'Telecommunications in Nigeria', University of Pennsylvania African Studies Centre, March 1996, Retrieved 25 July 2012 from http://www.africa.upenn.edu

Bello W, "China Eyes Africa: The New Imperialism? *Multinational Monitor,* Vol. 28 No.1, 2007, pp.23

Bukarambe B, Nigeria-China Relations: The Unacknowledged Sino-dynamics: in Ogwu, (ed), New Horizons for Nigeria in World affairs, Lagos: Nigeria Institute of International Affairs 2005, p 235
Brautigam D, China Africa and the International Aid Architecture, 2010 P.39.

Bbc news online, "China Pledges $ 20 Credit for Africa at Summit" Retrieved 28 December, 2012 from www.bbc.co.uk/news/world-asiachina-18897451

'Chinese telecommunication magnate to expand Nigerian market', Xinhua, 25 August 2011, Retrieved 26 July 2012 from http://news.xinhuanet.com

Cindy H, China's Oil Rush in Africa: Energy Security July 2006 p 10, Retrieved 24 Nov. 2012 from http://www.iags.org/chinainafrica.pdf

"China, Nigeria Sign Oil Development Agreement," China Daily, 19 December 2004<http://www.chinadaily.com/cn> Accessed August 18, 2012

CNBC, The world's 15 Biggest Oil Producers, retrieved from http://www.cnbc.com/id/41887743/The_World_s_15_Biggest_Oil_Producers?slide=7 10 December, 2012.

Choi, C.J. & Nailer, C. 'The China market and European Companies Prices and Surviving the local competition' *European Business Review*, 2005,' Vol. 17 No 2, pp. 177-190

---

[51] Brautigam D, China Africa and the International Aid Architecture, 2010 P.39.

E. Olawale OGUNKOLA, Abiodun S. BANKOLE & Adeolu ADEWUYI, China-Nigeria Economic Relations: Scoping Studies on China-Africa Relations, Trade Policy Research and Training Program (TPRTP) Ibadan, Nigeria, 2008

FOCAC: A Win-Win Formula for Sino-African Relations? 10th October, 2000. Retrieved November 15 2012 from http://www.thebeijingaxis.com/tca/editions/the-china-analyst-jan-2010/64

Geohive, Global Statistics/Population Statistics, 27 November, 2012, Retrieved from http://www.geohive.com/

Goldman Sachs, How Solid are the BRICs? Global Economics Papers No 134, 2005, p.8 retrieved from http://www.goldmansachs.com/our-thinking/topics/brics/brics-reports-pdfs/how-solid.pdf on 4 Dec. 2012

Gregory, M.S, *Elephant, Ants and Superpowers: Nigeria's Relations with China; South African Institute of International (SAIIA) Affairs, Perspectives Global Insight*, 2009, p.10

Harry Bradman, Africa's Silk Road: China and India's New Economic Frontier, Washington D.C: World Bank, 2007

Leonard K. Cheng & Zihui Ma, "China's Outward FDI: Past and Future," in Proceedings of the NBER (National Bureau of Economic Research) Conference on China's Growing Role in World Trade (Chicago: University of Chicago
Press, 2007, p. 5. http://nber15.nber.org/books_in_progress/china07/cwt07/cheng.pdf.

Margaret Egbula & Qi Zheng, China and Nigeria: A Powerful South-South Alliance, 2011, Sahel and West Africa club secretariat, 2011, pp. 7-8

Markusen J, "The Boundaries of Multinational Enterprises and the Theory of International Trade" *Journal of Economic Perspectives* 9: 1995, pp. 169-89

Nigeria', Paper submitted at a conference entitled "Sector-led growth in Africa and implications for development", Commissioned by UNIDEP and AFEA, November 2007 Retrieved 6 December 2012 from, http://www.unidep.org

Nigeria Needs $10 B Investment Annually for O&G Industry," Xinhua News Agency, 11 October 2004, <http://www.rigzone.com> Accessed 5 December 2012

Nigeria," Energy Information Administration, Country Analysis Briefs, November 24, 2012, from<http://www.eia.doe.gov>

Nargiza Salidjanova, Policy Analyst for Economic and Trade Issues, Going Out: An Overview of China's Outward Foreign Direct Investment, 2011, p 1 Retrieved 21 Nov. 2012 from http://www.uscc.gov/researchpapers/2011/GoingOut.pdf

Omar, Ndao Elhadji, "Investment and Trade between West Africa and China: The Senegalese Case" *Academic Journal of International Business Research, Vol. 11 No 1, 2012*

Pang, C. K., Robert, D., & Sutton, j., "Doing business in China – the art of war*?", International Journal of Contemporary Hospitality Management*, 10/7, 272–282, 1998.

Policy Insights, "From Old-Donor Debt Relief to Emerging Lenders in Africa" No. 57, 2008, http://www.oecd.org/dev/insights

Rafeeat Aliyu, Chinese and Indian Investment in the African Telecoms Sector, Consultancy Africa Intelligence, 2011, pp. 1-2

Strategic Direction, 'Selling of China's rich and not so rich Need to go beyond the luxury market' Vol. 21 No.6, 2005, pp. 5-7, 2005

See Huawei website http://www.huawei.com/africa/en/catalog.do?id=312 Accessed on 26 November 2012

Spring, A. & Jiao, Y, 'China in Africa: African Views of Chinese Entrepreneurship', in Sigue, S. (ed.) 'Global and Local Dynamism in African Business & Development', Proceedings of the *International Academy of African Business and Development (IAABD) Conference* at the University of Florida, Gainesville, USA, 20th– 24th of May, 2008

S.A Tella,L. A . Amaghionyeodiwe & B.A Adesoye, 'Telecommunications Infrastructure and Economic Growth: Evidence from Nigeria', Paper submitted at a conference entitled "Sector-led growth in Africa and implications for development", Commissioned by UNIDEP and AFEA, November 2007, Retrieved 25 October 2012 from http://www.unidep.org

Utomi, P, China and Nigeria. Washington, Center for Strategic and International Studies, 2008.pp. 42-44

Wang J, "What Drives China's Growing Role in Africa? " *IMF Working Paper*, Vol. 7, No. 211, 2007, p.8

Wang, J & Bio-Tchane A, "Africa's Burgeoning Ties with China", *IMF Finance and Development*, Vol. 45 No.1, 2008.